Through Her Eyes

Behind Her Smile

Beverly Sade

Through Her Eyes

Behind Her Smile

Contents

INTRODUCTION

Although I don't consider myself a poet, I've been writing poetry since elementary school. I always found it to be somewhat therapeutic. I felt compelled to write and dedicate this book to women and the young girls we're raising to be women. We go through so much while on this journey called life. I've had my share of failures, heartbreaks, and feelings of self-doubt. You should know you're not alone. There will be rainy days. You can either go through it or grow through it. I choose to grow through it. This book consists of four themes, love, loss, self-reflection, and self-love. It will take you on an emotional ride, forcing you to look in the mirror, find your true self, and shower her with love! I poured my heart and soul into these writings. If you feel a bit sad, doubtful, or unsure about the road you're taking, I hope that by the time you finish reading this book, you feel lighter, empowered, and have more clarity of who you are because, at the end of the day; you hold the key to your happiness, success, and future. Thank you for supporting Through Her Eyes Behind Her Smile.

LOVE

BEAUTIFUL SURPRISE

You're the one I didn't know I needed.
Like a strong wave that sweeps the shore, you
crashed into me so suddenly.
I knew I would love you for an eternity, long
before our eyes met.
It's because of you, I believe in miracles.
A true gift from heaven. My shining star.
A constant reminder of God's undying love
for me is what you are.
There is nothing in this world I wouldn't do
for you.
And if you were to ask me if you are the light
of my life, I'd answer, my dear sweet child;
it's true.

LOVE STORY

Birds are flying high, singing a harmonious
tune, and the color of love is painted in the sky.
The ocean waves dance beside us, as my eyes
stay pinned on you.
I must pinch myself; it all feels too good to be
true.
Loving you comes easy, believe me.
I can stay lost here forever.
Me, leave your side? Never.
I hope you're thinking what I'm thinking, and
if you ask me, my answer is yes.
You caress my heart and kiss my soul.
The kind of love we share is one untold.
I want this feeling for the rest of my life.
I'm wishing on a star you'd ask me to be your
wife.

COME AWAY WITH ME TONIGHT

There's just one thing I ask of you.
Come away with me tonight.
Let's wake up some place magical.
No more tears, no lies.
Just pretty, blue skies, where the sun always
shines.
Our hearts would combine, and we would
become one.
Come away with me tonight.
To the other end of the world.
Let's wake up safe in each other's
arms, while I get lost in your eyes.
I meet your gaze and tell you I'll
never stop loving you.
Not even in a million years.
There's just one thing I ask of you.
Come away with me tonight.

FOOLISH

It would be foolish of me to say
you love me.
Who am I to say you truly care?
Before I take this plunge from up this high,
is it safe to say you're mine?
You must know how I feel inside.
Like an erupting volcano, my feelings can
no longer hide.
I'm eager to dive into you, I can't control
myself.
Every minute with you brings me closer to
heaven.
I don't want anyone else.
I know that in love there's no guarantees, so
why am I falling for you so foolishly?

WHY DO YOU WEEP?

Tell me baby, why do you weep?
Her love is like poison, mine is
tender and sweet.
I know she hurt you, and the betrayal
cut deep.
But my love runs wider than any
ocean, deeper than the Bering Sea.
Can't you see there's no need to
worry with me?
I cherish you too much to ever bring
you misery.
Tell me baby, why do you weep?

INFINITE LOVE

I get so lost in you; I don't see anyone else.
I find joy in your laughter.
Sunshine in your smile.
If you go away, my days would be long.
Nights would be cold.
I'd miss you forever and my heart would ache
for an eternity.
I'd swim across the deepest ocean, if it'll bring
me closer to you.
I want to love you forever, but the more I
think about it…forever isn't long enough.
An infinite love is what I'm feeling.

WHENEVER, HOWEVER

Like a leaf swirling in the wind, I'm at
your mercy.
Like a cold drink on a hot summer day,
you soothe me.
I don't care where you take me, as long
as we're together.
Whenever, however, I'm okay with
whatever.
I don't care if you're here forever to see
this through.
All that matters is that in this moment,
I'm with you.
But if the wind happens to blow, and
you're no longer mine.
I could never regret you; you gave me an
experience of a lifetime.

CLOUD 9

If you're looking for me, you can find me
high up in the clouds.
Still floating on your love.
The way you make me feel, you must be
sent from up above.
You send me way up there.
I think I like it here.
I'm on a natural high.
I'm addicted to you.
I'm far too gone to turn back now.
So, hurry back my love.
I don't want to come back down.

WITH YOU

I walked into the room, confident as can
be, and without saying a word, you
gravitated toward me.
Days turned into months, and months
turned into years.
You've been by my side through it all.
You helped ease my fears.
Before you came along, I thought I'd
never trust again.
You look pass my physical, and really see
me from within.
I love you for loving me.
The good, the bad, even the ugly.
You make me do childlike things, like
carve you and me forever on the trunk of
an oak tree.
With you I can simply be myself,
phenomenally me.

WILDEST STORM

My sweet baby, I don't want to see you
cry.
Because you're hurting deeply, you want
to tell me goodbye.
You love me, and that scares you.
My sweet baby, what is a girl to do?
I won't hurt you the way she did.
This time around it won't be the same.
Take my hand, and let's dance in
the rain.
I can't let you slip away from me.
Dark skies, angry winds…we'll weather
them some day.
The wildest storm couldn't drive
me away.
By your side is where I vow to stay.

Sometimes the love is strong enough to survive all of life's phases. Other times it fades right along with its changes.

Like my fingertips riding the waves of the ocean, I can feel the intense shift. You no longer love me and this I know for certain.

LOSS

TWIN FLAME

I know you better than you know yourself.
I can feel you drifting away.
Your flame no longer burns for me, and it's
killing me to know.
You've found another, and she wants my spot.
It's only a matter of time before you go.
I know what you're thinking, so my eyes well
up with tears.
I beg and plead, but all you can say is that
you're not responsible for my fears.
You're wishing you were there, instead of
here.
Why is love so unfair?

HOW DO YOU DO THAT?

How do you do that thing you do?
Love so passionately, then flip the switch,
leaving me without a clue.
My mind is in shambles, looking for answers
I'll never find.
You said, God sent me to save you.
How could you be so unkind?
I was the one that dried your tears, rocked you
in my arms, and held you close to my heart.
How do you do that thing you do?
I keep thinking, you somehow erased me from
your memory. Is that true?
Please tell me, so then just maybe I can get
over you.

STILL WAITING

I said this time around I wouldn't fall, but
the walls I built easily crumbled.
Your words sweet like honey.
I hung onto them.
Said you were here to set me free.
My knight in shining armor.
So blinded by the lights, I couldn't see
past the facade.
Your words now bring pain and misery.
Still, I beg you not to set me free.
Your words are now broken promises.
Yet, I hang onto them.
Still hoping, still believing one day my
knight will return.

CATCH 22

It's time to move on.
Yes, I know.
My mind and heart are at war.
My mind knows what it is.
My heart is stuck on what it was.
It's time to move on.
Yes, I know.
So, I tell myself none of it was real.
You touching my soul deeply.
Your promises to never leave me.
Us making a house our home.
Maybe I imagined it all.
It's time to move on.
Yes, I know.
How can I move on, if I can't stop
loving you?

DAYDREAMING

Flowers came for me today.
There was a beautiful note attached.
It said, I'm sorry for everything.
I love you and every passing moment
without you is too much to bear.
Such a beautiful reminder.
I thought I slipped away from the corners
of your mind.
Now my heart's racing and my feet are
detached from the ground.
I'm eager to see you, embrace you and tell
you I feel the same, but then there's a
knock at my door.
Such a wicked reminder.
I was only daydreaming.

SPEAK NOW OR FOREVER HOLD YOUR PEACE

I've loved you for half my life.
It's kind of scary to imagine not being your wife.
I never thought we'd end up like this.
Us against the world are the days I miss.
Yes, we both lost our way and I don't want to play the blame game, but there's something I must say.
You took for granted that I'd always be there.
And I made up my mind that you just didn't care.
Battling in love & war left us both with scars.

Now we're standing at this bridge, both afraid to cross.
Are we going in different directions?
No matter what we decide, forever in my heart is where you'd reside.
And because of the life we built, I'll always think of you with pride.
We had a good run baby, you and I.
God only knows how hard we tried.
Speak now or forever hold your peace.
Is this our last and final goodbye?

SUMMER BLUES

The sun is cheerful.
The flowers have bloomed, but on
this bright and sunny day I'm still
blue.
I thought my tears would've dried by
summer.
I know now that until you return, my
days will be somber.

The truth is, it's not you that I miss. It's the idea of what we could've been that I cling to. And what's tearing my heart apart is that I can't help but wonder, who's loving you now.

WISHFUL THINKING

It was naive of me to think this breakup
would end peacefully.
As much as I want it to, anger still follows
me.
I'm annoyed at what you called love.
In a perfect world I'd forget about it all.
Cursed the day you walked into my life,
that cold December.
I wish more than anything that I didn't
remember.

RESENTMENT

No more taking the high road.
You left me with a broken heart and a
bunch of emotions to unload.
If I could go back in time, I'd never let
you into my world.
You suffered from low self-esteem, so
you made me your girl.
Needed me to feed your ego and I
obliged.
Your intentions were never pure and this
I know for sure.
I regret ever knowing you.
I don't want you ringing my phone,
wishing me well, and I've blocked you
from my social media too.

There is so much power in letting go. When you harbor bitterness and resentment in your heart, it eats away at your soul.

LOVE'S KARMA

Mama always told me you get
what you give.
And daddy always told me that when
people hurt you, let go and forgive.
Because in life everything comes back
around full circle.
With you, my heart and intentions were
pure.
You came in with a plot to allure me with
your illusions of love.
But one thing for certain, I'm favored by
the man above.
In that, I find peace.
As for you, karma you'll soon meet.

In love, you won't always win but even in the loss, there's so much to gain.

Let go of what is gone, open your heart
and embrace what is yet to come.

A DAY TOO LATE

I woke up today no longer wanting you.
I blocked your number and deleted every
text and picture.
I no longer need to hang onto those things.
So over the stress and anxiety it brings.
Looking back, I don't know what I saw in
you.
You're a womanizer, a narcissist and a
gaslighter too.
You made me question my own sanity, like
everything I felt wasn't true.
As if you didn't lie, didn't cheat, then flip
the script and put it all on me.
You blamed me for everything, even your
blatant disrespect.
Played the field for so long, but it's time I
intercept.
You can no longer play with me.
You're a day too late.
Go soak in your own misery.

SILVER LINING

I followed your lead, with my eyes wide
shut.
Too many bumps and bruises along the
way.
You took me out into the deep end and
left me drowning in my tears.
A lot of damage was done to my heart this
time.
Never again will I fall into love so blind.
I'd spot another you a mile away.
Mr. Casanova, the type to always know
what to say.
You made me think you were the prize.
Hahaha, how silly was I?
When I lost you, I found me.
It took nearly a year for me to see through
all the pain and misery.
It's because of you I'm a better ME.

And when they leave you hopeless and blue,
just know there is something greater on its
way to you.

LOVE BLOSSOM

I woke up this morning feeling brand new.
Like there was nothing in this world I
couldn't do.
The sun shined heavily through my
windowpane, and I could hear the birds
singing, "Lovely Day."
What a perfect time to say goodbye to
yesterday.
I've held on way too long, but today I'm
singing a new song.
The sight of the apples blooming on
the tree, lets me know that something special
is on the way to me.
I knew it was only a matter of time before the
storm passed.
I can feel the love in the air once again, at
last.
Summer is my favorite season again.

SELF-REFLECTION

TIMES LIKE THIS

I didn't know my heart was so heavy until
someone spoke of his name.
Suddenly, I couldn't hold back the tears, and
the pain hurt the same.
The same as it did, the day he tore my world
apart.
Bruised my spirit, and shattered my belief in
love.
All I truly want is a fresh, and clean start.
But I locked away my feelings and put them
on a shelf.
And more than anything, I want to come
home to myself.
Where I'm safe. Where I'm loved. Where
I'm whole.
And it's times like this, I need to trust my
inner guidance and hear my soul.

Sometimes you don't know you need healing until you're triggered, and suddenly you're hit with all sorts of feelings. To move past the hurt, you must be willing to face it. And most importantly, embrace it. If you have unanswered questions, now is the time to ask yourself because the answers lie within you.

LONG ROAD HOME

Will I ever reach my destination?
Feels like a never-ending road.
Just keep going, one day you'll make it,
are the words I've been told.
I've been traveling for some time.
I'm afraid I'll soon grow weary.
I'm losing this battle in my mind.
My days are dreary.
Have I made a wrong turn?
Have I missed any signs?
What is God trying to show me?
Am I not reading between the lines?
I prayed for an angel to guide me.
Still, I'm lost and confused, entirely.

HELLO SADNESS

My never-ending black moon.
I didn't think you'd be back so soon.
Last time you were here, I drowned in my
sorrow.
I said farewell to hope like there is no
tomorrow.
Why won't my happiness last?
Is God punishing me for something I've
done in the past?
I've been moving at the speed of light,
going nowhere fast.
And my ending comes too soon.
My never-ending black moon.

MIRROR

Mirror mirror, on the wall.
Tell me the meaning behind it all.
Why am I attracting men that only subtract
from me?
Look into my eyes, then tell me
what you see.
Is it my lack of self-love, or insecurities?
I crave a deep love that's fulfilling.
I think it's time I look at myself, and do
some healing.
No more putting band aids on old wounds,
trying hard to cover what's inside.
I'm going beneath the surface this time,
using my soul as a guide.

A GIRL I ONCE KNEW

She was a delicate flower, but now she's
grown wild.
She never felt her mother's love.
Her daddy deemed her a bastard.
Out searching for love in all the wrong
places.
Her scent of desperation attracts wicked
faces.
They only want to use her. Pick her apart.
Because of her parents, she was doomed
from the start.

JUSTINE

Justine, she's just sixteen…trying to find
her way in a world so mean.
Caterpillar, turned wounded butterfly,
unknowingly chasing evil in disguise.
All she wants is to be loved.
All she wants is to feel.
She climbs in and out of random beds, for a
temporary feeling that isn't real.
All that matters is that in that moment, she
belongs somewhere.
A piece of her is left behind each time.
Too many miles, a lot of wear and tear.
Justine, you're just sixteen…if no one else
does, just know that I care.

IN TIME

Growing up in a system; so broken.
Buried words of pain unspoken.
Ashamed and alone, your crowded house is
not a home.
If only somehow you could fly away.
Close your eyes and envision how you'll live
someday.
No matter how dark your start, keep a pure
heart.
I promise you this is not your end.
Positivity, prayers and love I send.
In time, you'll rise above all and transcend.

HURDLES

Time keeps ticking.
My feet keep moving, yet I stand still.
No matter how ugly things get, I believe
there's beauty waiting on the other side of the
hill.
I have to keep going. I have to keep climbing.
Then maybe tomorrow, I'll see things
aligning.
But if tomorrow comes and I'm still standing
here, that won't turn me away.
I'll keep going because I know I'll make it
over this hill someday.

SILENT STORM

Today I had a setback.
Those thoughts crept back into my mind.
Will I make it? Am I good enough?
Will I discover my true purpose in time?
Today I don't feel hopeful.
Those dark clouds are forming.
I thought I moved passed the storming.
But tomorrow is another day.
I'll reset in the morning.

RAINY DAYS

Everyone loves the sunshine, but what
happens when it rains?
Will you run and hide for shelter?
Bury your feelings, and hope things get
better.
What will I do? I won't fight against the
weather.
I'm standing out in the rain.
I want to wash away the pain.
I'll come out shiny and new.
Clean heart, mind and spirit too.

It's those rainy days that force me to truly look at myself. And I've realized that my reflection has never been so clear.

THE UNKNOWN

There will come a time when you'll question
everything about yourself.
You'll wonder if you're doing enough.
You'll ask yourself, what's my purpose?
You'll question your life's direction.
These uncertainties are sometimes needed
for us to grow.
Embrace these moments, and confidently
welcome the unknown.

BLURRED REFLECTION

You may look in the mirror and
not recognize the reflection staring back at
you.
Life spun a web, and you don't know what
to do.
Each way you turn, you find yourself
trapped.
You throw your hands in the air, and decide
to adapt.
Now there's a chip on your shoulder and
it's weighing you down.
Pick yourself up and adjust your crown.
Don't miss your blessings, being bitter and
stuck on yesterday's lessons.

You are what you believe you are. Your thoughts become reality. "I can" and "I will" should always be your mentality.

NO EXIT

There's something in my way.
Heaven knows I've tried to shake
what's blocking my path.
Visions flash before my eyes.
I pray this blockage won't last.
I reach the top of the mountain,
only to be pulled down fast.
Heaven knows I'm trapped.
God has shown me the way out.
My escape is mapped.
I see the light at the end of the
tunnel, but then it fades to black.
There's something in my way that
pulls me right back.

You can either go through it or grow through it.

EXIT HERE

In this well of darkness is when you truly
learn yourself.
The only voice that echoes is your own.
If you feel there's something holding you
back, maybe there are parts of you that
need to stay behind.
Nothing is ever wasted, you're exactly
where you need to be.
Search within yourself and find that inner
lock and key.

INNER MAKEOVER

Being alone is not the same as being lonely.
And starting over does not equate to failure.
You're weak and unworthy are the lies they
tell you.
You start seeking validation.
Knocking on doors with no answer.
Didn't anyone tell you that you hold the key?
Trust your own vision and not what others see.
Dig deep within yourself and refurbish your
roots.
You'll find that true happiness lies within you.

PITFALL

Thanks to you, I'm writing again.
Thanks to you, I see clearly now.
Thanks to you, I'm looking at me.
Thanks to you, I recognize my mistakes.
Thanks to you, I'm doing what it takes.
Thanks to you, I found strength within.
Thanks to you, I won't fall again.

Sometimes pain is our greatest teacher.
It's through those experiences that we
learn our most important lessons.

SELF-ABANDONMENT

I've made you feel worthless.
Like the last doll on the shelf.
The last piece of nothing that's left.
I stopped loving and needing you.
When I felt low with no one to turn to, it was
you that got me through.
You were my light in the darkness.
The sun that peaked through cloudy skies.
I wreck my brain trying to understand why.
Why, I strayed.
By your side is where I should've stayed.
How could I ever forgive myself for
abandoning you?

FINALLY FOUND

There was a girl named Faith, who
once was lost.
Men were blinded by her beauty, and her light
that shined so bright.
They only wanted to experience her.
Not love her for a lifetime.
Faith's light starts to flicker with time.
She wants to be loved.
She wants someone that she can call her own.
She keeps chasing, only to find herself all
alone.
She began seeing herself through the eyes of
those who picked her up and threw her away.
Drifting through life on empty.
Lost, and confused.
Where is Faith?

You see, she had given so much of herself, she
had nothing left to give.
Her light flickers and flickers, till it's out.
She's in the dark and can't find her way.
Faith dropped to her knees and prayed one
day.
Tears streamed down her face, as she
whispered, "God, please show me the way.
I've made a lot of wrong turns in my life,

and I don't know where I'm going.
Please, just show me the way."
Faith began to pray every day and every night.
While in her darkness, and in her solitude,
something magical happened.
She began to see the light again.
She heard a stern voice say, "pull yourself
together. Everything you need is inside of you.
Stop chasing. Stop searching. Know yourself,
then learn to love yourself, and you will attract
an abundance of love."
At the end of the day…it all goes back to
YOU.

SELF-LOVE

BLACK BIRD

Black bird, you're such a rare beauty.
You're special and unique in every way.
And whenever I hear you sing, I know it's
going to be a glorious day.
What I'm trying to say is…
Why do you compare yourself to the
others?
Their feathers bloom of bright color, but
none of them stand out the way you do.
Black bird, black beauty, you hold the key
to that magical door.
Black bird, spread your wings and soar.

FALSE TRUTH

You ever have someone make you feel like
you weren't good enough?
Their uncertainty of you makes you feel less
of a woman.
Like you're second best.
The shame of not being chosen over
someone else begins to burn a hole
in your chest.
This is when self-doubt, self-hate and
insecurity begins.

WOMAN VS GIRL

You're a woman, stop comparing yourself
to that girl.
You're deep in your feelings, because
suddenly he wants to leave your world.
He didn't choose her because she's better
than you.
He chose her because with you, you see
right through...
The lies and empty promises.
You ask those questions that force him to
look at himself.
A boy posing as a man can only pretend for
so long.
With you, he must come correct.
You demand respect.
With her, all those things he can neglect.

And I've learned, you should never go out
of your way to prove to someone that
you're enough. Anyone that doesn't
recognize or appreciate your worth,
doesn't deserve you.

You may not understand why some people walk out of your life. Trust that everything happens for a reason. Once you enter your new phase, it will all make sense why they had to go.

WANDERER

Float on floater.
You've got lessons to learn.
True unconditional love, you can't discern.
Float on, there's mistakes to be made.
It will be confusing at first, but be unafraid.
Just know that you'll find your center
again.
But first, you've got to love yourself...that's
when your glow up will begin.

SUDDENLY

A budding flower doesn't need another flower
to bloom.
All it needs is the love in the sky.
Sailboats make their way through great seas.
All it needs is the love in a breeze.
Trust that everything you need in life comes
naturally.
And suddenly, you realize you don't need
another person to complete you.
You don't need approval from others.
All you need is the love in the sky.

Stand strong like a tree and leave behind any parts of yourself that seek validation from others.

NEW WOMAN, WHO'S THIS?

The nerve of you to show up at my door six
months later.
The same door you walked out of without
saying goodbye.
I cried myself to sleep night after night.
I would've given anything to feel you again
and have you here in my reality.
But it's a new day, and I'm not who I used
to be.
Disloyal lover, your absence made me
stronger.
Time and time again you've shown me how
cruel your love can be.
My heart doesn't hold a space for you any
longer.
All I've got inside is unconditionally for
me.

They'll be back when they fail at replacing you, or when they need you to feed their ego. This is your time now. Feed your soul and let them go.

INTERMISSION

Weren't you the one who told me I'd be
nothing without you?
I replayed those words in my mind so
much I believed they were true.
I suffered from a shortage of self-love
supply.
I thought you made me whole, so I
painfully held onto you and me.
You said I would crumble if I ever told
you goodbye.
But without you the sun is still bright.
The stars still peak out at night.
And I'm not that fragile person that was
so easily broken.
I'm standing stronger than ever before.
I'm all I'll ever need and more.

SELF-RECOVERY

I used to think I needed a new lover to repair
my heart and recover.
A different character, but same script.
I go back to the beginning, hurt and stripped.
Stripped of my dignity, self-esteem and pride.
Chasing city lights with nowhere to hide.
As of now, I'm on a self-care spree.
Every single one of you were undeserving of
me.
For the first time in my life, I'd rather be
alone.
There's a rainbow glistening somewhere for
me.
I can do this on my own.

BOOMERANG

It all starts and ends with you.
You hold the power in each and every
way.
Know that the seeds you plant will
manifest someday.
The best way to show someone how to
love you, is by deeply loving yourself.
What you put out into the universe; it
finds its way back.
If you love yourself wholeheartedly, a
magnetic love you will attract.

HEALING NATURE

If anyone asks, tell them I went for a walk.
I don't know when I'll return.
I don't want to cry these tears anymore, my
soul; it burns.
I need to feel the grass beneath my feet.
I need to be kissed by the sun.
I have a lot of releasing to do, and I'm not
leaving here until I'm done.
Like me, these trees have many feelings.
A bird told me you heal best in a room with no
ceilings.
If anyone asks, tell them I went for a walk.
Nature and I are having a talk.

It's never too late to become the best version of yourself.

SAILING ON

I'm moving on to a place where I can be
free.
To a place where I can unveil myself and
truly be me.
I just need to feel the fresh air and let my
skin breathe.
Too many people value what's superficial.
I'm searching for what's beneath.
That's where the true beauty lies, like the
rose that grew from concrete.

UNDERNEATH IT ALL

Canceling my hair appointment today.
I'm getting rid of my hair straighteners and
blow dryer too.
Saying bye to my lashes, extensions and hair
glue.
Removing these false nails and if HE
doesn't like it…then, oh well.
I like me better underneath it all.
Underneath it all, there's so much beauty to
see.
Naturally, unapologetically me.

WAYS

An extrovert on some days.
An introvert on most.
When it comes to social media, I rarely
post.
Protective of my energy, I can't just let
anyone into my space.
I guess you can say I'm somewhat weird in
my own way.
I prefer to do my own thing and not ride the
popular wave.
I don't aspire to be anyone else but me; I'm
my own fave.

FLAWLESS

Jumping up and down, trying to squeeze
into these jeans.
Mama said there isn't much I can do about
my wide hips; it's in our genes.
Today I'm going to flaunt these curves by
any means.
I haven't left the house much since I gave
birth.
It's been even longer since my husband
touched me; I almost forgot my worth.
I had to remind myself who I am and
embrace my new body.
I've got stretch marks and cellulite that run
deep.
And still, I love me.

FAREWELL FRIEND

We started at Double Dutch, corner store
runs, and playing dress up for fun.
You're the only one that knows where my
secrets lie.
Remember our pact? "We're going to grow
old together, you and I."
I couldn't have gotten through my first
heartbreak without you.
And when your dad died, a piece of me did
too.
When you cried, I cried.
We were real sisters.
We owned our high school hallways.
I can't help but smile, reminiscing.
Those were the days.

Childhood living was so much easier to do.
As time went on, I became too ambitious
for you.
You settled in life, yet you told me I was
reaching too high.
Friend or foe now circles my mind, and I
can't understand why.

Who am I fooling? That's a lie.
I understood clearly what was brewing
inside you.
You loved me, but the envy and jealousy
tipped the scale.
It hurts that it's come to this, but I'm
saying farewell.

Love yourself so much that you don't hesitate to let go of things, people, or situations that are not in alignment with your self-growth.

BET ON YOU

Have you looked in the mirror lately?
Do you know how capable you are?
No? I'll remind you.
Time and time again, disaster has struck.
You've weathered every storm.
You healed your heart when it was broken
into a thousand pieces.
When you felt lost in the crowd, you found
your own way.
You rise above it all, day by day.
If there's one person you can count on, it's
you.
Things change, people change.
Life can be a fickle thing.
Roll the dice and bet on you.

Never be ashamed of where you've
been. Look in the mirror and smile at
your progress. Then, focus on where
you're going.

RENAISSANCE WOMAN

You can be a devoted mother and still chase
your dreams.
You can be a student and a teacher.
A wife and a lover.
You can have class and still be sexy.
You can be sour and sometimes sweet.
You are not stone.
On any given day, you can be whatever you
want to be.
You are forever evolving, like the colors on
a leaf.

Don't let people tell you who you are, and where you're going. If you're not careful, you'll stop your growth without knowing.

SUPERMOM

You roll over at 6:00 a.m. to shut off your
alarm.
You didn't get much sleep because you were up
all night soothing your newborn.
You quickly shower, dress, then rush to the
kitchen to make breakfast for five.
More and more these days, it's hard for you to
feel alive.
Because you're always on the go for the ones
you love.
You're a wife, mom, and businesswoman,
carrying the weight of things you never speak
of.
Because you wear an S on your chest.
Strength, resilience, and confidence are some of
the qualities you possess.
You're a diamond that shines in the darkest
hours.
A true supermom who deserves her flowers.

You've earned the right to toot your own horn. Celebrate yourself because no matter how tough life gets, you show up every day and get the job done!

EXPENSIVE

You can't afford to give up.
The price is too expensive.
And you're way too ambitious for that talk.
You've given your all to this dream and now
you're ready to walk?
I know it's hard to see your life past where you
are right now.
Trust that the stars are aligning and your
breakthrough is on the horizon.

NOBODY LIKES TRAFFIC

More than ever, you're feeling the pressure.
Comparing yourself to what you see online
makes you think you don't equally measure.
Trying hard to keep up is wearing you thin.
Your self-confidence is slipping from within.
There's too much traffic in that lane.
Why don't you maneuver over?
You'll get to where you're going a lot sooner
if you stop following the crowd.
Look in the mirror and say these words out
loud.
My only competition is me, and I'm going to
make myself proud.

Don't lose yourself; in a world full of illusions. Stay focused and in your own lane. Move at your own pace. Your life journey should not feel like a race.

RIVERS

Like water just let it flow…
Because no one can take away what's
truly yours.
Keep your mind at peace, even when
facing closed doors.
You've had your share of setbacks; this I
know.
But sometimes the lesson is found in the
detour.
Our struggles make us stronger; it also
gives us perspective.
Know that your hard work and
perseverance will prove to be effective.
Like water just let it flow, because no one
can take away what's truly yours.

HIGH VIBRATIONS

Welcome, come inside.
Everything is everything over here.
Good thoughts are dancing perfectly in
my head.
Those days of letting the world get the
best of me are dead.
I'm leaving the ashes of yesterday to
fall behind.
Because I know eternal sunshine I'll
someday find.

UNTITLED

There will always be someone that
doesn't believe in you.
There will always be someone who
doesn't appreciate your worth.
There will always be someone that
deserts you.
There will always be someone who
tries to break your spirit.
But that someone should never be
you.

CLARITY

Because I'm a woman now, I can see
things clearly.
I know my worth, and I don't need anyone
to validate me.
Because I'm a woman now, I realize that
some people come into your life only for a
season.
Still, there will always be a reason.
It's usually to help you grow.
Because I'm a woman now, I realize that
my past does not own me, nor does it
define me.
I've learned to let those things go.
Because I'm a woman now, I don't need a
man to feel whole.
I can be alone and not feel lonely.
I find comfort in being on my own.

MESSAGE IN THE SKY

I once wrote a letter to myself and gave
it up to the sky.
I'll tell you a secret, but you must keep
it between you and I.
I asked God for the things I wanted.
Then I thanked him for them as if they
were already mine.
My intentions were set.
I continued to work on my personal
growth, my goals and let the universe do
the rest.
The message that was sent to me
couldn't have been more clear.
Because of my positive affirmations,
success and fulfillment were near.
Such a beautiful message to receive.
Confirmation that magical things
happen; when you simply believe.

SOULFUL AFFIRMATIONS

I am Blessed.
I am Loved.
I am Worthy.
I am Self-Sufficient
I am Enough.
I am Creative.
I am Intelligent.
I am Beautiful.
I am Confident.
I am Striving
I am Thriving
I am getting better and better; each
and every day.

WOMAN TO WOMAN

Dear Woman,

You've been through many ups and downs,
but you remained solid through it all. You
were able to find your light in the darkest of
times. Every obstacle that has come your way,
you held onto your faith and saw it through.
That's not an easy thing to do, especially when
you feel there's no one cheering for you.
When people told you that you failed because
your dreams got derailed, you saw the forest
for the trees. Always remember, you're
enough. You're all you'll ever need. In life,
there are no guarantees, but when you believe,
closed doors open, eventually. Now, a new
level is on the horizon, and this is your season
to bloom. If no one else has told you, let me
be the first to say, I'm so very proud of you!

Love Always,

Beverly Sade

Photo Credit: Keith Major

Beverly Sade is an actress, author, and entrepreneur. She has appeared in numerous popular television and film projects. Beverly is an avid writer who has contributed to the works of many authors. In 2009, Beverly's debut novel was released. Since then, she's authored two best-sellers. She is the owner of The Beverly Company and Beverly Sade Publications. *Through Her Eyes Behind Her Smile*, is her 4th book release.

www.ingramcontent.com/pod-product-compliance
Lightning Source LLC
LaVergne TN
LVHW011337080426
835513LV00006B/393